S0-BXW-740

BEST PRACTICES IN STUDENT CENTERED LEARNING

A PLANNING, RESOURCE AND REFERENCE WORKBOOK IN THE DEEPER LEARNING WORKSHOP SERIES

ENGAGEMENT, INNOVATION AND IMPACT BY DESIGN

PRINCIPAL AUTHOR:
Charity Allen

Produced by
PBL Consulting
936 NW 57th St
Seattle, WA 98107

Please contact
PBL Consulting at
www.pblconsulting.org,
360-440-3968 or
charity@pblconsulting.org
for more information.

GRAPHIC DESIGN BY:
Charity Allen

www.pblconsulting.org

WORKSHOPS FOR DEEPER LEARNING
TABLE OF CONTENTS

STUDENT CENTERED LEARNING

RESPONSIVE TO A LEARNER'S
1. CURRENT LEVEL OF PERFORMANCE
2. LEARNING NEEDS, STYLES & PREFERENCES
3. PERSONAL INTERESTS, STRENGTHS,
CHALLENGES, GOALS & PASSIONS

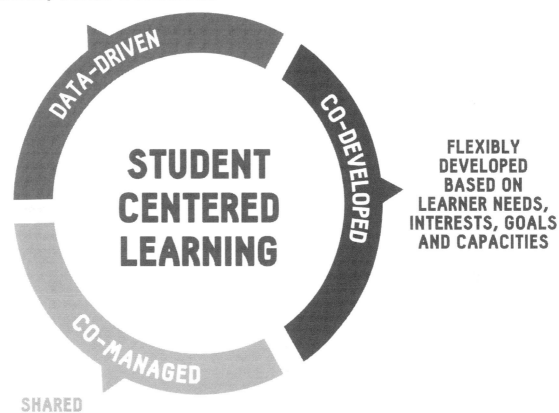

DATA-DRIVEN

CO-DEVELOPED

CO-MANAGED

STUDENT CENTERED LEARNING

FLEXIBLY
DEVELOPED
BASED ON
LEARNER NEEDS,
INTERESTS, GOALS
AND CAPACITIES

SHARED
(1) PROGRESS MONITORING
(2) CREATION OF LEARNING PATHWAYS
(3) CREATION OF ASSESSMENT PATHWAYS

OBJECTIVES	To review the spectrum of best practices for Student Centered Learning. To craft a personalized plan to further your professional practice with Student Centered Learning best practices, strategies & more.
DRIVING QUESTION	How can we increase student agency in learning?
MAJOR DELIVERABLES	• Personalized Learning Plan • Learning Profile • Goals & Action Plan
ASSESSMENT	Student Centered Learning Student Criteria Student Centered Learning Teacher Criteria
RESOURCES	Use our online space to access resources including: texts, protocols, videos, materials, samples and more. Also, check out these resource-rich websites: *www.pblconsulting.org*, *www.nextgenlearning.org,* *www.edutopia.org, www.bie.org, www.hightechhigh.org*, *www.eleducation.org, and www.nsrfharmony.org*.

NOTES

Driving Question: How can we increase student agency in learning?

Agency is defined by one Wikipedia article ("Agency", n.d., para. 1) as:

"Agency is the capacity of an entity (a person or other entity,...) to act in any given environment." The article goes on to say that, "human agency is the capacity for human beings to make choices."

So to paraphrase in this context, student agency would be the capacity of a student to act or make choices in a given environment. Let's return to the Driving Question: How can we increase student agency in learning? Student agency in learning can be increased through two key pathways, in a multitude of specific ways.

Pathway 1:

Increase one's capacity to act as an agent.

Pathway 2:

Increase conditions that enable agency

WHAT ARE SOME WAYS TO INCREASE STUDENT AGENCY IN LEARNING?	
IN PATHWAY 1:	IN PATHWAY 2:

STUDENT CENTERED LEARNING
STUDENT CRITERIA

AS A STUDENT, I...	ALMOST ALWAYS	OFTEN	SOME-TIMES	RARELY OR NEVER
FEEL LEARNING IS PERSONALIZED				
I feel encouraged to learn and show my learning in a variety of ways. I can do this because I have access to the tools and materials I need, based on my goals, my needs, my learning style and preferences, my interests and my capacities.				
KNOW ABOUT MYSELF AS A LEARNER				
I know my current levels of academic performance. I am aware of my learning style and my learning preferences. I recognise my strengths and challenges. As I continue learning, these understandings help me make choices about how, when, with whom, with what and where I learn.				
UNDERSTAND MY LEARNING GOALS				
I can access and explain learning outcomes that I need to meet. These include academic learning outcomes in my courses as well as goals in my areas of interest. I propose and develop learning goals that are important, interesting and unique to me.				
CHOOSE MY LEARNING PATHWAYS				
Independently, I can use a variety of pathways to learn. I know about the different learning pathways that are available to me. I can select the best learning pathway based on my learning goals, my current levels of performance as well as my learning style and preferences. I use these pathways to develop knowledge, skills, understandings and competencies. Learning pathways include self-teaching, working with peers and experts, teacher-guided instruction, digital & hardcopy resources, online programs, MOOCs, internships, projects and more.				
MONITOR MY PROGRESS				
I know how to check in with my progress. I use a variety of ways to determine how I'm doing with my learning goals. I can adjust my learning pathways, as needed, to achieve my learning goals. I track and record my progress. When I am ready, I demonstrate how I have accomplished my learning goals.				
PARTICIPATE IN MY LEARNING COMMUNITY				
In my learning community, we learn together. I learn and I also help others (including adults) learn. Sometimes I feel like a student and sometimes I feel like a teacher. I share and demonstrate my learning. Adults teach and learn alongside me.				

AS A TEACHER, I...	ALMOST ALWAYS	OFTEN	SOME-TIMES	RARELY OR NEVER
PROMOTE PERSONALIZATION				
Explicitly and implicitly, I promote personalization. I build culture, spaces, materials and processes that enable learners to learn and demonstrate their learning in a variety of ways, based on their unique goals, interests, learning style, needs and preferences as well as their current and potential capacities.				
USE LEARNER DATA				
I facilitate awareness for learners about their current levels of performance in relationship to established and co-constructed learning goals. I promote meta-cognition for learners about themselves-as-a-learner. This includes surveying, assessment and reflection about their learning style, their learning preferences as well as their strengths and challenges. This helps the learner independently make choices about how, when, with whom and where they advance their learning.				
BUILD TRANSPARENCY WITH LEARNING GOALS				
I use a variety of materials, tools and processes to ensure established learning outcomes are clear and accessible for learners. I work individually with students to co-construct learning goals that are unique to them based on their personal needs, abilities and interests. This includes developing and actively using personalized learning plans.				
FACILITATE MULTIPLE LEARNING PATHWAYS				
In advance and in response to learner needs and requests, I design, develop, create, broker, collect and/or make available a variety of learning pathways. I make available multiple instructional components for a given learning outcome to be accessed and used by different learners with varying needs, learning styles and preferences as well as levels of performance.				
PROMOTE MULTIPLE ASSESSMENT PATHWAYS				
As appropriate for the learning outcome or goal, I design, develop, create, broker, collect and/or make available a variety of pathways to measure, determine and enable demonstration of how learners are performing in relationship to established and co-constructed learning outcomes and goals. I check in with how learners are performing and can recommend adjusting learning pathways, as needed, to help learners achieve their learning goals.				
MODEL WITHIN THE LEARNING COMMUNITY				
I practice what I preach. I develop and communicate my own learning goals, pathways and progress. I share new learning, when and to whom it's relevant. This may include conducting action research and sharing findings.				

Student Centered Learning
is tailored to individual learners based on how they learn, their current levels of performance as well as their personal interests and goals.

Using Learner Data

Student centered learning begins when we take the time to learn about the learners themselves. This includes facilitating learner meta-cognition and reflection on themselves as learners. Data is collected and used to support this process. Using a variety of approaches, some schools compile this data into a Learner Profile that is revisited and revised regularly. Typically, this process includes the following data points:

- current levels of academic performance
- learning needs & styles
- learning preferences
- personal interests, strengths, challenges, goals, passions, etc.

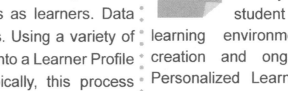

Student Designed & Influenced Projects

Some schools practicing PBL have moved from teacher-designed, unit-based project based learning to either student-influenced or even to student-designed projects. This could include Maker Spaces, Tinkering & Genius Hour. This shift is aimed at increased personalization, motivation and engagement. Several school models around the U.S. have been using this approach to PBL for years, and even decades. For more information, samples, videos and more, visit the websites for the following organizations: Summit Public Schools, Edvisions Schools and Big Picture Schools.

Personalized Learning Plans

A key practice in student centered learning environments in the creation and ongoing use of Personalized Learning Plans or PLPs for each student. PLPs outline the established and co-constructed goals (both academic and personal) for students. PLPs are revisited often with each student to check in on how they are progressing to meet their short and long-terms goals. During meetings, new goals and action items are tailored to each student to support goal achievement.

Flexible Spaces

Given the potential that students will be pursing different learning goals, in different ways, flexible spaces enable variability in learning pathways for each student.

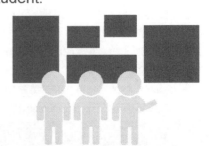

Blended Learning
is an approach that incorporates both face-to-face and online components, with some choice given about how, where, when, how fast and with whom one learns.

Digital & Online Media

A variety of high quality media is available and used in blended environments to enhance learning and shift how face-to-face time is used. Instructional videos can also be created and shared.

Adaptive Learning Programs

Adaptive Learning Programs that respond to user progress & performance and enable competency-based advancement. They are considered adaptive as well as student-centered because they tailor themselves to the user's current level of performance.

Flipped Classroom

This strategy can help shift the way classroom time is used. "One-size-fits-all" instruction, such as lectures, are shared with students digitally and often done as homework. In this way, class time can be used for small group instruction, application tasks, personalization & more.

Flexible Instruction

Student Experts

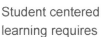

Student centered learning requires shifts in how we think about instruction. Teachers can't clone themselves after all. One approach is to leverage students' unique skills and capacities and invite them to lead instruction, consult with individuals and groups & more.

Protocols

To foster learner capacity for independent learning, equip them with effective learning processes, including protocols. If learners can pull from a repertoire of protocols, then they can more easily pursue independent and group learning, with less direct teacher guidance.

Gamification of Learning

While the name is deceiving, gamification does not typically involve playing "video games." Rather principles of game design, such as leveling up, quests, missions, leader boards, and more are incorporated into a brick and mortar classroom for mostly non-digital learning.

Stations

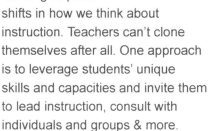

Stations, centers and the use of the rotational model are all structures to enable learners to pursue different learning pathways, at different times and in different ways.

Learning Menus

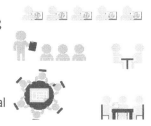

Various instructional components aligned to various learning targets can be developed and provided to students as a "playlist of learning" from which learners can self-select based on their goals and preferences.

Flexible Grouping

Various grouping arrangements can be used based on the targeted learning goals, as well as students' learning styles and preferences. Flexibility is key.

DAY-TO-DAY COMPONENTS

MY PERSONALIZED LEARNING PLAN

MY LEARNING GOALS

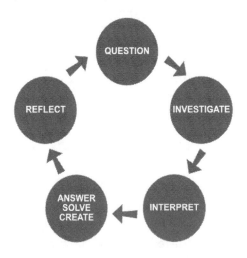

Just as students are unique learners, adults too have different learning styles, learning preferences, areas of strength and challenge, as well as goals and aspirations.

Therefore, adults too should learn about themselves as learners, set professional goals, select different learning pathways, monitor their progress and actively participate in the learning community, both in the role of learner and in the role of teacher.

Use the Personalized Learning Plan and Learning Profile Templates to set some goals to guide your learning today and beyond.

PERSONALIZED LEARNING PLAN

NAME:	DATE:	ROLE/ASSIGNMENT:

MY LEARNING GOALS

QUESTIONS / WONDERS	SMART GOALS / ACTION STEPS
Conduct preliminary research in response to your questions and wonders to determine what to pursue actionably and in greater depth.	☐ Plan for, practice and reflect on a new strategy ☐ Find a collaborator / mentor / expert to work alongside ☐ Plan and conduct an action research project ☐ Conduct a book study ☐ Other:

MY GOAL PARAMETERS

WITH WHOM	WHEN & BY WHEN	WHERE

WHY: WHAT I HOPE TO LEARN / ACCOMPLISH	RESOURCES NEEDED	OTHER CONSIDERATIONS

LEARNING STYLES & PREFERENCES

APPROACH TO WORK & INTERACTING WITH OTHERS

STRENGTHS	CHALLENGES

LEARNING PREFERENCES *(rank options in each category with 1 being your first/top preference)*

LEARNING ENVIRONMENTS

In my environment, I learn best with/when...

Noise Levels
☐ Silent ☐ Noisy ☐ Music Playing ☐ Other:

Activity / Movement
☐ Activity Around Me ☐ No Movement ☐ Other:

Temperature
☐ Warm ☐ Cool ☐ Other:

Light
☐ Well lit ☐ Dim ☐ Lights Off ☐ Other:

Work Space
☐ Sitting ☐ Standing ☐ Lounge ☐ Other:

Other Environmental Considerations:

TEAMING & TIMING

I prefer learning...
☐ On My Own
☐ With a Partner
☐ With Peers In Small Groups
☐ With Peers On Mid-Large Size Teams
☐ In Diverse Committees
☐ Within My Professional Learning Networks
☐ Through Expert Mentorship
☐ Other:

When it comes to time, I prefer learning in the...
☐ Morning ☐ Afternoon ☐ Evening ☐ Night
☐ Other:

MODALITY FOR LEARNING

I prefer learning through...
☐ **Reading**
☐ **Listening** (lectures, podcasts, audiobooks, etc.)
☐ **Watching** (media, demonstration, modeling, etc.)
☐ **Peer Collaboration** (peer dialog, discussion, etc.)
☐ **Mentorship** (apprenticing, one-on-one instruction, etc.)
☐ Other:

MODALITY FOR SHARING MY LEARNING

I prefer sharing my learning through...
☐ **Writing** (reports, essays, white papers, etc.)
☐ **Explaining** (lectures, podcasts, verbal exchanges, peer dialog, etc.)
☐ **Showing Digitally** (video, media, graphical epresentations, etc.)
☐ **Showing In Person** (demonstration, modeling, etc.)
☐ Other:

MY CURRENT LEVELS OF PERFORMANCE

STRENGTHS WITHIN MY ROLE

☐ Using Learner Data
☐ Personalized Learning Plans
☐ Student Driven Project Based Learning
☐ Flexible Spaces
☐ Blended Learning
☐ Flexible Instruction
☐ Other:

AREAS FOR GROWTH IN MY ROLE

☐ Using Learner Data
☐ Personalized Learning Plans
☐ Student Driven Project Based Learning
☐ Flexible Spaces
☐ Blended Learning
☐ Flexible Instruction
☐ Other:

STUDENT DRIVEN PBL

Some schools practicing PBL have moved from teacher-designed, unit-based project based learning to either student-influenced or even to student-designed projects. This could include Maker Spaces, Tinkering & Genius Hour. This shift is aimed at increased personalization, motivation and engagement. Several school models around the U.S. have been using this approach to PBL for years, and even decades. For more information, samples, videos and more, visit the websites for the following organizations: Summit Public Schools, Edvisions Schools and Big Picture Schools.

WHY DO I WANT TO PURSUE THIS PARTICULAR PRACTICE / STRATEGY?

WHERE AM I CURRENTLY WITH THIS PRACTICE / STRATEGY?

WHAT DO I HOPE TO LEARN / ACCOMPLISH?

WHAT IMPACT COULD THIS LEARNING HAVE ON MY STUDENTS' GROWTH?

WHAT QUESTIONS / WONDERS DO I HAVE?

HOW CAN I EXPLORE INTEGRATING THIS PRACTICE?

☐ Plan for, practice and reflect on a new strategy
☐ Find a collaborator / mentor / expert to work alongside
☐ Plan and conduct an action research project
☐ Conduct a book study
☐ Other:

(Use Action Plan Template)

INQUIRY LOG

QUESTIONS	SOURCE	WHAT I LEARNED	NEXT STEPS

LEARNING MENU

STUDENT DRIVEN PBL

 Big Idea: I involve students in creating pathways for learning and demonstration of learning.

Objectives	Pathways for Learning & Demonstration of Learning
I involve students in a project design process to co-develop learning opportunities aligned to students interests, needs, learning outcomes and goals.	• Review sample projects and video, audio or text based experiences of teachers and students using student-designed PBL. • Develop a plan to involve students in a codesign process for PBL. • Review, adopt and/or adapt sample processes for student-designed PBL.
I develop and use processes through which students can develop their own learning opportunities aligned to their interests, needs, learning outcomes and goals.	• Review video, audio or text based experiences of teachers and students using student-designed PBL. • Review, adopt and/or adapt sample processes for student-designed PBL.
I develop and use processes support the alignment of learning opportunities and projects to learning outcomes and track learner achievement.	• Review case studies and from other schools regarding ways to promote competency based advancement. • Review programs and processes for tracking student achievement in nonlinear ways. • Develop a clear plan and revise as needed.

Student Driven PBL

Interact with this learning menu digitally at www.pblconsulting.org

STUDENT DRIVEN PBL

 Big Idea: I involve students in creating pathways for learning and demonstration of learning.

Possible Sources	Activities
Sample Projects: www.pblconsulting.org **Sample Projects:** BIE's Project Search Engine **YouTube Channel:** Big Picture Schools **Video:** Student-Influenced PBL at Summit PS	• **Consider & respond:** How do different systems achieve student influenced PBL? What can you learn and implement from their model?
Publication: Edvisions Program Overview **Book:** The Coolest School in America **Sample:** Edvisions Student Driven Project Planning Process for Students **Video:** Edvisions - The Evolution of a project.	• **Consider & respond:** How do different systems achieve student driven PBL? What can you learn and implement from their models? • **Application Task:** Develop tools, templates and/or materials from scratch or that you adopt or adapt.
Website: Show Evidence **Website:** Project Foundry **Video:** Student View of PLPs at Summit PS. **Video:** Teacher View of PLPs at Summit PS.	• **Consider & respond:** How could Show Evidence or Project Foundry support competency based advancement, non-linear progress, multiple student pathways as well as monitoring progress and achievement? What other options could work?

A **GLOBAL** COMPONENT
OF STUDENT CENTERED LEARNING

USING LEARNER DATA

Student centered learning begins when we take the time to learn about the learners themselves. This includes facilitating learner meta-cognition and reflection on themselves as learners. Data is collected and used to support this process. Using a variety of approaches, some schools compile this data into a Learner Profile that is revisited and revised regularly. Typically, this process includes, but is not limited to, the following data points:
Current levels of academic performance, learning needs & styles, learning preferences, personal interests, strengths, challenges, goals, passions, etc.

WHY DO I WANT TO PURSUE THIS PARTICULAR PRACTICE / STRATEGY?

WHERE AM I CURRENTLY WITH THIS PRACTICE / STRATEGY?

WHAT DO I HOPE TO LEARN / ACCOMPLISH?

WHAT IMPACT COULD THIS LEARNING HAVE ON MY STUDENTS' GROWTH?

WHAT QUESTIONS / WONDERS DO I HAVE?

HOW CAN I EXPLORE INTEGRATING THIS PRACTICE?

☐ Plan for, practice and reflect on a new strategy
☐ Find a collaborator / mentor / expert to work alongside
☐ Plan and conduct an action research project
☐ Conduct a book study
☐ Other:

(Use Action Plan Template)

INQUIRY LOG			
QUESTIONS	SOURCE	WHAT I LEARNED	NEXT STEPS

LEARNING MENU
USING LEARNER DATA

 Big Idea: I collect, organise and use data about learners.

Objectives	Pathways for Learning & Demonstration of Learning
I can develop, select, adopt or adapt metrics, tools & processes to gather information about learners, including data about one or more of the following: • current levels of academic performance • learning needs & styles • learning preferences, personal interests, strengths, challenges, goals, passions, etc	• Review, select, adopt or adapt potential metrics on which to collect and use data. • Review, select, adopt or adapt tools and materials (surveys, inventories, assessments, etc.) used for data collection.
I can compile data on learning needs, styles and preferences into a Learner Profile for which I have developed, selected or adapted a template/format.	• Review, adopt or adapt sample Learning Profiles. • Develop a plan to organize and archive data in a way that's functional for all users.
I can plan and structure time to discuss collected data with learners and I can prompt thoughtful and useful reflection and support data-driven action.	• Investigate best practices in goal setting and conferring with learners. • Develop a plan with a framework for discussion, goal setting and reflection.
I plan the best ways and frequency at which to revisit and revise this Learner Profile collaboratively with the learner to monitor progress and to ensure it is current and accurately evolving as the learner grows and progresses.	• Review case studies and from other schools regarding ways and frequencies to actively use a Learner profile. • Discuss and reach agreement on a continuity of practice internally. • Develop a clear plan, revise as needed.

Using
Learner Data

Interact with this learning menu digitally at www.pblconsulting.org

Big Idea: I collect, organise and use data about learners.

Possible Sources	Activities
• **Article**: Are your grades really giving you information on your students' levels of performance? • **Sample:** Learning Style Compass Inventory • **Sample:** Learning Style True Colors Inventory • **Sample:** Learning Preferences Inventory A • **Sample:** Learning Preferences Inventory B	• **Consider & respond:** On which metrics should you collect data? • **Application Task:** Develop tools, templates and/or materials from scratch or that you adopt or adapt. • **Consider & respond:** How can you ensure you're getting accurate data on academic levels of performance of students?
• **Sample:** Learner Profile Template A • **Blog & Samples:** Overview and 4 Templates • **Video:** Experience using Learner Profiles	• **Application Task:** Develop tools, templates and/or materials from scratch or that you adopt or adapt.
• **Wikipedia Article:** SMART Goals • **Edutopia Blog:** Goal Setting with Students • **Publication**: Conferencing with Students • **Article:** Using Data in the Classroom • **Publication:** Using PLPs & Learner Profiles • **Video:** Learner Profiles at Edvisions	• **Consider & respond:** What are the best ways to confer with different types of learners? How frequently? • **Consider & respond:** How, when and at what frequency will you frame discussions, goal setting and reflection? • **Application Task:** Develop tools, templates and/or materials from scratch or that you adopt or adapt.

STUDENT CENTERED LEARNING
FLEXIBLE SPACES

Given the potential that students will be pursing different learning goals, in different ways, flexible spaces enable variability in learning pathways for each student. Spaces might include, computer labs, collaboration centers, individual work stations, lecture halls, tech-rich labs, Makers Spaces and more. In this way, work for a variety of purposed can be pursued individually or in teams with greater ease.

WHY DO I WANT TO PURSUE THIS PARTICULAR PRACTICE / STRATEGY?

WHERE AM I CURRENTLY WITH THIS PRACTICE / STRATEGY?

WHAT DO I HOPE TO LEARN / ACCOMPLISH?

WHAT IMPACT COULD THIS LEARNING HAVE ON MY STUDENTS' GROWTH?

WHAT QUESTIONS / WONDERS DO I HAVE?

HOW CAN I EXPLORE INTEGRATING THIS PRACTICE?

☐ Plan for, practice and reflect on a new strategy
☐ Find a collaborator / mentor / expert to work alongside
☐ Plan and conduct an action research project
☐ Conduct a book study
☐ Other:

(Use Action Plan Template)

INQUIRY LOG			
QUESTIONS	SOURCE	WHAT I LEARNED	NEXT STEPS

FLEXIBLE SPACES

 Big Idea: I develop, use and make available a variety of spaces responsive to variability with purposes, tasks, teams, learning pathways and more.

Objectives	Pathways for Learning & Demonstration of Learning

Objectives

I conceptualize, select, fund, repurpose, develop, normalize usage and periodically improve a variety of spaces intended to be responsive to variability with purposes, tasks, teams, learning pathways and more. Spaces may included any of the following, and more:

- Collaboration Spaces
- MakerSpaces
- Individual Work Stations
- Specific Function Spaces
- Multi-function Spaces
- Labs
- Lecture Halls
- Media Centers
-

Pathways for Learning & Demonstration of Learning

- Select the space to be used for a given purpose.

- Investigate best practices in space design to optimize the functionality and the feeling for the space.

- As needed, seek out funding pathways to optimize the space for its purpose.

- When appropriate, enlist stakeholders fund, develop and optimize the space.

- Develop or co-develop norms for the space.

- Agree on an internal plan for space usage that benefits all stakeholders.

- Develop an instructional plan that scaffolds the use and norms of this space, if new for learners.

- Develop a plan for periodic improvement of the space.

Flexible Spaces

Interact with this learning menu digitally at www.pblconsulting.org

Big Idea: I develop, use and make available a variety of spaces responsive to variability with purposes, tasks, teams, learning pathways and more.

Possible Sources	Activities
Space Design: **Video:** Designing for Student Centered Learning **Video:** The dSchool as a Case Study **Video:** The dSchool's approach to space design **Article:** Questions to ask when setting up a MakerSpace **Video:** Architects Collaborate on Space Design **Book:** Make Space by Stanford's dSchool	• **Application Task:** Conduct a modified gap analysis protocol: The protocol document prompts you to discuss belief in relationship to practice. To modify the protocol, discuss the current spaces in relationship to the vision or in relationship to best practices in optimizing the space. • **Application Task:** Develop a plan to scaffold use of the space, including developing or co-developing norms.

STUDENT CENTERED LEARNING
PERSONALIZED LEARNING PLANS

A key practice in student centered learning environments in the creation and ongoing use of Personalized Learning Plans or PLPs for each student. PLPs outline the established and co-constructed goals (both academic and personal) for students. PLPs are revisited often with each student to check in on how they are progressing to meet their short and long-terms goals. During meetings, new goals and action items are tailored to each student to support goal achievement.

WHY DO I WANT TO PURSUE THIS PARTICULAR PRACTICE / STRATEGY?

WHERE AM I CURRENTLY WITH THIS PRACTICE / STRATEGY?

WHAT DO I HOPE TO LEARN / ACCOMPLISH?

WHAT IMPACT COULD THIS LEARNING HAVE ON MY STUDENTS' GROWTH?

WHAT QUESTIONS / WONDERS DO I HAVE?

HOW CAN I EXPLORE INTEGRATING THIS PRACTICE?

☐ Plan for, practice and reflect on a new strategy
☐ Find a collaborator / mentor / expert to work alongside
☐ Plan and conduct an action research project
☐ Conduct a book study
☐ Other:

(Use Action Plan Template)

INQUIRY LOG			
QUESTIONS	SOURCE	WHAT I LEARNED	NEXT STEPS

LEARNING MENU
PERSONALIZED LEARNING PLANS

 Big Idea: I help learners set short and long terms goals and monitor progress and achievements.

Objectives	Pathways for Learning & Demonstration of Learning
I can compile learner data, reflections and goals into a Personalized Learning Plan for which I have developed, selected or adapted a template/format.	• Review, adopt or adapt sample PLPs. • Review experiences of teachers and students using PLPs. • Develop a plan to organize and archive data in a way that's functional for all users.
I can support thoughtful goal setting around both established learning outcomes and co-constructed goals that are unique to the individual.	• Investigate best practices in goal setting and conferring with learners. • Develop a plan with a framework for discussion, goal setting and reflection.
I can plan and structure time to discuss collected data with learners and I can prompt thoughtful and useful reflection and support data-driven action.	• Investigate best practices in goal setting and conferring with learners. • Develop a plan with a framework for discussion, goal setting and reflection.
I plan the best ways and the frequency at which to revisit and revise Personalized Learning Plans collaboratively with the learner as well as with stakeholders in order to monitor progress, to ensure the PLP is current and to modify as needed so that the PLP accurately evolves as the learner grows & progresses.	• Review case studies and from other schools regarding ways and frequencies to actively use PLPs. • Discuss and reach agreement on a continuity of practice internally. • Develop a clear plan and revise as needed.

Personalized Learning Plans

Interact with this learning menu digitally at www.pblconsulting.org

PERSONALIZED LEARNING PLANS

 Big Idea: I help learners set short and long terms goals and monitor progress and achievements.

Possible Sources	Activities
Sample: 11th Grade PLP, 6th Grade PLP, MS PLP, Kinder PLP, **Video:** Student View of PLPs at Summit PS. **Video:** Teacher View of PLPs at Summit PS.	• **Consider & respond:** Which tools, templates and/or materials will you adopt or adapt? Or will you develop your own?
Wikipedia Article: SMART Goals **Edutopia Blog:** Goal Setting with Students **Publication:** Conferencing with Students **Video:** Reflections on Building Habits of Success at Summit PS. **Video:** Student-Advisor Relationships at Edvisions	• **Consider & respond:** What are the best ways to confer with different types of learners? How frequently? • **Application Task:** Develop tools, templates and/or materials from scratch or that you adopt or adapt.
Publication: Using PLPs & Learner Profiles **Expert Input:** Carol Dweck weighs in on PLPs **Video:** A day in the life of a student at Summit PS **Video:** PLPs at Edvisions	• **Consider & respond:** To what extent does one's learning style/preferences change over time? • **Application Task:** Develop a plan for how, when and at what frequency you will frame discussions, goal setting and reflection.

A **GLOBAL** COMPONENT
OF STUDENT CENTERED LEARNING

STUDENT CENTERED LEARNING

BLENDED LEARNING

Blended Learning is an approach that incorporates both face-to-face & online components, with some choice given about how, where, when, how fast and with whom one learns. With Blended Learning, teachers can cherry-pick from the array of strategies to gain the maximum benefit:

1. *Blending in* **Online and Digital Media**, such as Khan Academy, TEDed, YouTube, Crash Course, Lynda.com, MOOCs and more. Why reinvent the wheel in developing a delivering a lecture or a lesson when extremely high quality versions are readily available? To a some extent, it's likely that most teachers are already integrating online and digital media. Therefore, to some degree, they are already "blending." To what degree are you blending? Could additional blending provide additional value?

2. *Blending in* **Adaptive Online Learning Programs** (AOLPs) *in addition to* face-to-face instruction and activities. This is the equivalent of a Spanish teacher using Duolingo or Rosetta Stone, *in addition to* the normal class instruction and activities. With Blended Learning, one might add and incorporate them, not substitute them for high quality classroom instruction.

3. *Blending in* **the Flipped Classroom Approach** simply means, to some degree, a teacher may assign elements from the aforementioned two strategies (using digital & online media and AOLPs) as well as instruction that is "one-size-fits-all" (lectures, direct instruction, etc.) to be done as homework instead of as class work. Traditionally, one-size-fits-all instruction is provided at school and students are sent home to "make sense of the material" on their own. Flipping affords the teacher the precious class time to engage learners in a variety of interactive activities, applications tasks as well as small group and individualized instruction.

WHY DO I WANT TO PURSUE THIS PARTICULAR PRACTICE / STRATEGY?	WHERE AM I CURRENTLY WITH THIS PRACTICE / STRATEGY?
WHAT DO I HOPE TO LEARN / ACCOMPLISH?	**WHAT IMPACT COULD THIS LEARNING HAVE ON MY STUDENTS' GROWTH?**

WHAT QUESTIONS / WONDERS DO I HAVE?

HOW CAN I EXPLORE INTEGRATING THIS PRACTICE?
- ☐ Plan for, practice and reflect on a new strategy
- ☐ Find a collaborator / mentor / expert to work alongside
- ☐ Plan and conduct an action research project
- ☐ Conduct a book study
- ☐ Other:

(Use action plan template)

INQUIRY LOG			
QUESTIONS	SOURCE	WHAT I LEARNED	NEXT STEPS

BLENDED LEARNING

 Big Idea: I use both face-to-face and online learning components, with some choice given about how, where, when, how fast & with whom one learns.

Objectives	Pathways for Learning & Demonstration of Learning
Online & Digital Media: I select, organize and make available to learners multiple learning and instructional resources from a variety of online and digital sources.	• Review video, audio or text based experiences of teachers and students using online & digital media. • Review, select, organize, align to learning outcomes and make available resourcesfrom key databases.
Adaptive Online Learning Programs (AOLPs): When appropriate, I incorporate AOLPs into daily and unit-based face-to-face classroom instruction.	• Investigate best practices in gamification. • Develop a lesson plan that gamifies your targeted learning outcomes.
Flipped Classroom: I determine which digital/online resources could/should be used on-demand and which resources ought to be done by all learners - I assign the later, as appropriate.	• Audit existing face-to-face components to ensure they are interactive, engaging and application-based tasks / activities. Assign others to be done out of class.
Online & Digital Media / Flipped Classroom: I determine which digital/online resources will complement the existing face-to-face classroom components of a course.	• Conduct analysis of existing curricular scope and sequence to align new digital/online resources, as is relevant to the learning outcomes.
Online & Digital Media As much as would advance learning, I make available "one-size-fits-all" direct instruction and lecture components in a digital format to be used on-demand and as directed by teacher.	• Select, develop and/or make available digital versions of the "one-size-fits-all" direct instruction and lecture components.

Blended Learning

Interact with this learning menu digitally at www.pblconsulting.org

Big Idea: I use both face-to-face and online learning components, with some choice given about how, where, when, how fast & with whom one learns.

Possible Sources	Activities

Possible Sources

Samples:
- Khan Academy
- TEDed
- YouTube
- Crash Course
- Minute Physics
- Lynda.com
- iTunesU

Website: Edu App Rating Database
Sample: Duolingo - World Language AOLP
Sample: iXL - Math AOLP
Video: Math teachers uses a variety of programs

Video: Intro to the Flipped Classroom
Video: The Flipped Classroom Model
Publication: The Flipped Classroom Guide

Your Curriculum Documents
Printed Samples: Useful Protocols for interactivity in the classroom in Workshop Workbook
Samples: Giant Bank of Protocols

Blog: How to make your own instructional videos
Tutorial: Create a lesson using TEDed
Video Tutorial: Ways to make your own videos
Sample:

Activities

- **Application Task:** Create a list of links to all the videos or lessons relevant to one or more of your courses.
- **Application Task:** Plan how, when and to whom to offer flipped lesson(s.)

Application Task: Using Graphite, attempt to find the best AOLPs for your course. Consider whether or not, and how, to use them.

- **Consider and respond:** In what cases would the Flipped Classroom Approach work or not work in your course?
- **Application Task:** Plan a flipped lesson.

- **Application Task:** As appropriate, align existing curricular outcomes to relevant digital/online resources.
- **Application Task:** Plan a flipped lesson.

- **Consider and respond:** What are your most effective and engaging lectures/lessons students love? Create a list.
- **Application Task:** Make a digital version of your best lesson(s.)

STUDENT CENTERED LEARNING

FLEXIBLE INSTRUCTION

Flexible instruction moves away from the type of planning in which one may design a given lesson with instruction, activities, tasks, assessments and reflections intended to be completed by all students, in more-or-less, the same order. Flexible instruction plays out a lot like it sounds - it is planned, developed and intended to provide learners with choice about how, where, when, how fast and with whom one learns. There are many specific strategies that enable the larger practice of flexible instruction, including: (1) Learning menus, (2) stations/rotational model, (3) flexible grouping, (4) gamification of learning, (5) building learners' independent capacity with key protocols and (6) cultivating and leveraging student expertise.

WHY DO I WANT TO PURSUE THIS PARTICULAR PRACTICE / STRATEGY?

WHERE AM I CURRENTLY WITH THIS PRACTICE / STRATEGY?

WHAT DO I HOPE TO LEARN / ACCOMPLISH?

WHAT IMPACT COULD THIS LEARNING HAVE ON MY STUDENTS' GROWTH?

WHAT QUESTIONS / WONDERS DO I HAVE?

HOW CAN I EXPLORE INTEGRATING THIS PRACTICE?

☐ Plan for, practice and reflect on a new strategy
☐ Find a collaborator / mentor / expert to work alongside
☐ Plan and conduct an action research project
☐ Conduct a book study
☐ Other:

(Use Action Plan Template)

INQUIRY LOG			
QUESTIONS	SOURCE	WHAT I LEARNED	NEXT STEPS

FLEXIBLE INSTRUCTION

 Big Idea: I use a variety of instructional strategies flexibly to align to learner levels of performance, needs, interests, preferences and more.

Objectives	Pathways for Learning & Demonstration of Learning
Student Experts: I inventory students for their existing areas of strength and, as appropriate, I leverage the use of their strengths for peer learning.	• Review, select, adopt or adapt potential metrics on which to collect and use data. • Review, select, adopt or adapt tools and materials (surveys, inventories, assessments, etc.) used for data collection.
Protocols: I scaffold the use of a bank of protocols for discussion, tuning work, reflection, problem solving, reading and discussing texts, mediation, etc.	• Select protocols that are relevant to your course and age of students. • Develop an instructional plan to scaffold their use.
Gamification of Learning: When appropriate, I incorporate principles of game design into daily and unit-based face-to-face classroom instruction.	• Investigate best practices in gamification. • Develop a lesson plan that gamifies your targeted learning outcomes.
Stations: I develop multiple instructional components that can be used by some or all students, at the same or different times, using an on-demand, flex or rotational model.	• Investigate best practices in stations / centers / rotational models. • Develop an instructional plan that scaffolds the use of this approach, if new for learners. • Select, develop, adapt or adopt instructional components that can be used in a station context.

Flexible Instruction

Interact with this learning menu digitally at www.pblconsulting.org

FLEXIBLE INSTRUCTION

 Big Idea: I use a variety of instructional strategies flexibly to align to learner levels of performance, needs, interests, preferences and more.

Possible Sources	Activities
Blog: "Leveraging Students for their own success" **Video:** Students leading lessons **Publication:** Students as teachers for tech **Article:** Leveraging Student Experts in Tech	• **Consider & Respond:** What types of expertise do your students have that could be relevant in a student centered learning environment? • **Application Task:** Plan to inventory student for strength and build/use expertise.
Printed Samples: Useful Protocols for interactivity in the classroom in Workshop Workbook **Samples:** Giant Bank of Protocols	• **Application Task:** Select protocols that are relevant to your course and age of students and or/ develop an instructional plan to scaffold their use.
Article: The Hows and Whys of Gamification **Case Study:** Blog & videos of a 11th grade physics teacher who gamified.	• **Application Task:** Gamification can be done at a big, unit-based scale or a small, daily-lesson-plan scale. Decide how far down this rabbit's hole you'd like to explore.
ASCD Publication: Rotation Models **Video:** The Flex Model **Video:** The Lab Rotation Model **Video:** The Station Rotation Model	• **Consider and respond:** What do you notice about the different models? In what cases would this work or not work for you? • **Application Task:** Plan a lesson, or series of lessons, that incorporate stations with the most relevant model - flex, lab rotation or station rotation.

FLEXIBLE INSTRUCTION

Big Idea: I use a variety of instructional strategies flexibly to align to learner levels of performance, needs, interests, preferences and more.

Objectives	Pathways for Learning & Demonstration of Learning
Learning Menus: I develop menus of learning pathways with activities, resources, media and more that are aligned to learning outcomes that can be used by some or all students, at the same or different times, using an on-demand, a flexible or an assignment-based approach.	• Align learning outcomes to resources, activities and media. • Develop an instructional plan scaffolds the use of this approach, if new for learners.
Flexible Grouping: I allow and/or assign a wide variety of team structures depending on the learners and on the nature of the task/objective.	• Investigate guidelines, best practices and research in various teaming structures. • Consider learner needs & preferences and audit your course to determine when various teaming structures are most relevant.

Flexible Instruction

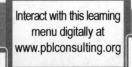

Interact with this learning menu digitally at www.pblconsulting.org

Big Idea: I use a variety of instructional strategies flexibly to align to learner levels of performance, needs, interests, preferences and more.

Possible Sources	Activities

Learning Menus: You're looking at one ☺

- **Consider and respond:** In what cases would the Learning menus work or not work in your course? How does this align to Blended Learning & the Flipped Classroom?
- **Application Task:** Develop a Learning Menu for your course. Plan to scaffold its use.

Edutopia Blog: Heterogeneous vs homogeneous
Edutopia Blog: "From Groups to Teams"
Research: What's the right size?

- **Consider and respond:** In what cases would various teaming structures work best?
- **Application Task:** Develop a menu of teaming structures and when you might use them.

A *DAY-TO-DAY* COMPONENT OF STUDENT CENTERED LEARNING

Formative Critique, Tuning & Assessment

WHACK-A-MOLE PROTOCOL

Place student work, along with criteria, critique instructions and/or questions for reflection, at student desks and/or stations. Students move around, as space is available, to provide critique for multiple pieces of work.

The idea is that they pop up when they finish each critique, like a mole in the "Whack-A-Mole" game. Then, they pop back down in a new spot to conduct another critique, wherever one is available. This works well when the amount of time it will take to conduct critique will predictably vary.

EXIT SLIPS

Prepared in advance by the teacher or done on-the-fly, exit slips can act as a check for understanding and/or collect information on work completion, effectiveness of instruction, process, materials, and more.

CHARETTE PROTOCOL

This protocol was typically used in engineering. It is best used early on to feed-forward, rather than back. As soon as a process stalls, students can call a "charette" to get fresh perspectives and ideas on how to move their project forward.

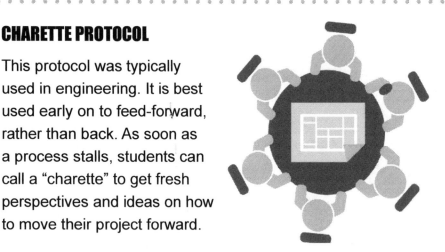

PAIR CRITIQUE

Students are paired with a critique partner. Pairs respond directly to critique and feedback questions generated by the teachers, the class and/or by the work author or designer.

2 STARS & A WISH

Students can acknowledge and share 2 things that were done well. Then they share a wish they have that would enhance the work being examined.

Formative Critique, Tuning & Assessment

GALLERY WALK

Text-lite work is hung in a space to mimic a"gallery." Participants walk the gallery and offer written feedback (often on Post-It Notes) in response to a prompt and/or using generic critique language.

INSTRUCTIONAL CRITIQUE

The teacher (or students) lead a small group or the whole class in the critique of one or more work samples to distil the quality indicators of said work. E.g. Thesis statements. The indicators can then be used to assess the students' work in progress. E.g. Students' draft thesis statements.

DILEMMA PROTOCOL

Student(s) present a dilemma, e.g. getting stuck, encountering a tricky problem, writer's block, etc. and protocol participants offer constructive feedback about how to respond to the dilemma.

ABC OF A TEXT

Create a acronym, each letter asks students to look for something specific in the work being examined.
e.g. SLUG
    S - Spelling
    L - Letter Formation
    U - Uppercase (first letter of first word in sentence)
    G - Greatness (what's great about the work)

DESIGN THINKING AND THE ENGINEERING DESIGN CYCLE

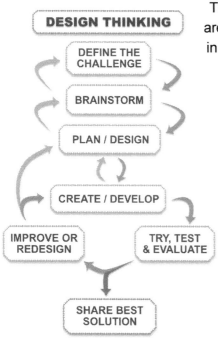

These two methods of inquiry are fairly similar. They are used in the adult world by designers and by engineers to conceptualize, plan, create and improve new "things" that have value.

Increasingly, teachers, students and schools at all levels are using these methods, which are already common in industry, to frame a process for making and creating.

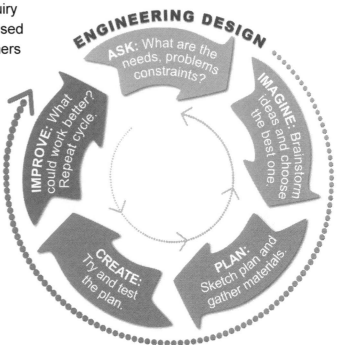

Generally speaking, the Engineering Design Cycle is used to create structures, systems, machines, engines & code. Design Thinking handles everything else.

SCAMPER

As a unifying strategy, try using this mneumonic device to confirm or improve the strength of an idea in progress or that is near completion.

S ubstitue something

C ombine it with something else

A dapt something to it

M odify or magnify it

P ut it to some other use

E liminate something

R eserve or rearrange it

MODELING

Teach students to use a variety of modeling tools to model systems, concepts or ideas. MIT experts say modeling is a new essential skill.

Examples:

- Model zoo enclousre prototypes using Sketchup
- Create short story prewrites using FreeMind or BubbleUs
- Model a biome using Kodu
- Model numberfactors using Excel

FOR DISCUSSION & REFLECTION

SOCRATIC SEMINAR

A strategy for text-based discussion and building background knowledge, this strategy helps us to build deeper understanding through text-based discussions and questionning. It can also be useful in teaching and practicing communication and discussion techniques, language and strategies. The two formats below represent how to physically structure the discussion. Multiple modifications are avaialable.

FORMAT A : PILOT & WINGMAN

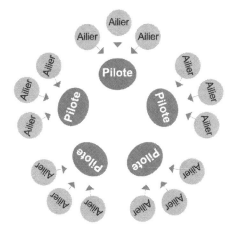

FORMAT B : FISHBOWL

SOCRATIC SMACKDOWN!

Socratic Smackdown was developed by the Institute of Play and is described by them as, "a versatile discussion-based humanities game to practice argumentation around any text or topic..." While they state that the game is designed for grades 6 through 12, many elementary teachers use it as well. They go on to say that , "it is a unique multiplayer game in which students learn how to discuss challengeing topics while competing to earn points. Because earning points is done through using discussion strategies and language, it creates an opportunity to have fun, discuss an issue and practice how to discuss well. Materials and tutorials can be downloaded for free at the Institute for Play's Website: www.instituteofplay.org

PHILOSOPHICAL CHAIRS

This strategy helps students form a position on an issue. They decide if they agree or disagree with a statement (or they take a side on an issue.) Then they arrange themselves by position physically within a space. Both sides on the position discuss the issue. Students can change their position on an issue and physically move to the other section.

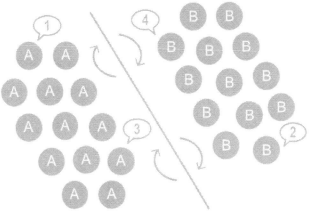

Rules: (1) One person speaks at a time. (2) The discussion. moves from Side A to Side B evenly. (3) Individuals may speak more than once, but they must let others on their side speak before contributing again. (4) If/when one changes position, they change sides physically. This can take place during the protocol.

41

FISHBOWL

The protocol uses two concentric circles to create an inner circle and an outer circle. The protocol can be used for discussion or reflection. Those seated in the inner circle discuss a topic or prompt and those seated in the outer circle listen, observe, take notes or complete other designated tasks. Often an empty seat is placed in the inner circle. This "hot seat" modification can allow multiple outer circle participants to join the inner circle discussion temporarily.

3, 2, 1

You can write any 3 questions or prompts. Students provide 3 responses to the first, 2 to the second and one to the final. Usually the first question or prompt is easier and lends itself to multiple responses and the final question or prompt is more complex.

CHALK TALK

In this protocol, a word, phrase, question or prompt is written on a chalk board (or white board or butcher paper, etc) and in silence students approach the chalk board and respond in writing. Their responses can connect to the initial prompt or they can connect directly to other responses. Multiple students can respond simultaneously. Students can respond multiple times. It ends when it ends. The entire protocol is silent.

SUCCESS ANALYSIS PROTOCOL

This protocol is all about determining cause and effect. When someone experiences a profound success, this protocol can help uncover that which led to the success. i.e. cause and effect. The idea is that through the identification and analysis of causal factors, promoting subsequent "successes" will be more likely. Learn more about how to conduct this protocol at www.nrsfharmony.org

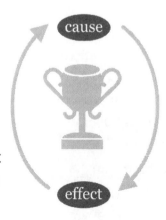

FOR DISCUSSION & REFLECTION

WORLD CAFE

In this protocol for discussion, each table is assigned a topic, with a discussion prompt. Participants select the table and topic of their choice and discuss the topic and prompt for 5-10 minutes. Participants switch tables 3-4 times, selecting their top topics. It can feel a bit like "musical chairs," but with enough rotations, one usually gets their top choices of topics by the end. At each table, using chart or butcher paper, groups attempt to create a visual representation of their discussion, with minimal usage of words. Groups review and build on previous discussion visuals and share their final one.

CONTINUUM DIALOG

This protocol could be adapted to be used with students for discussion or reflection. In this protocol,

an affirmative and negative statement are posed. Participants physically stand on a continuum. The continuum is indicated physically in the room as an arc in order for all participants to see where others place themselves. Placement on the continuum reveals participants' positions in

QUESTIONS FOR REFLECTION

Common questions could include:

1. What have you learned from doing this project?

Content	Process

2. On a scale of 1-4, how difficult was this project? Explain...
3. What have you learned about yourself?

As A Learner	As A Team Member

4. What would you do differently in future projects and why?

themselves on the continuum the facilitator can ask them to explain (2 mins or less) why they placed themselves where they did. No rebuttals, no arguments, no judgment.

As participants listen and hear different perspectives, they can physically move themselves in the event that their perspective shifts.

Learn more about how to facilitate this protocol at www.nrsfharmony.org

WHAT'S YOUR PLAN?

Now that you have a preliminary Personalized Learning Plan and Learning Profile, you can use those tools as a springboard for developing goals, action items and more.

Review the Action Plan Template and provided Sample Action Plan to respond to the questions below in an effort to guide your next steps.

OBSERVE

> **WHAT ARE YOU NOTICING ABOUT THE STRUCTURE OF THE FORM?**

> **REVIEW THE COMPLETED SAMPLE PLAN ON THE SUBSEQUENT PAGES. WHAT ARE YOU NOTICING?**

EXPLORE

> **WHICH GOALS AREAS ARE YOU DRAWN TO? WHY? IN PURSING THAT GOAL AREA, WHAT DO YOU HOPE COULD BE LEARNED AND ACCOMPLISHED BY YOU AND YOUR STUDENTS?**

DECIDE

> **WHICH GOAL AREAS WILL YOU EXPLORE IN GREATER DEPTH? IF POSSIBLE, ELABORATE ON A SPECIFIC PRACTICE OR STRATEGY IN THAT GOAL AREA.**
>
> ☐ Using Learner Data
> ☐ Personalized Learning Plans
> ☐ Student Influenced/Designed PBL
> ☐ Flexible Spaces
> ☐ Blended Learning
> ☐ Flexible Instruction
> ☐ Other:
>
> *(Ready to get started? Use the subsequent pages with logs, questions and forms to guide your work)*

ACTION PLAN TEMPLATE

NAME:	DATE:	ROLE/ASSIGNMENT:

MY LEARNING GOALS

GOAL AREA		SPECIFIC STRATEGY OR PRACTICE
□ Using Learner Data □ Personalized Learning Plans □ Student Driven Project Based Learning □ Flexible Spaces	□ Blended Learning □ Flexible Instruction □ Other:	

PLAN

WHAT AM I GOING TO DO?	WHEN AM I GOING TO DO IT?	WHERE AM I GOING TO DO IT? (COURSE, SECTION, CONTEXT)
□ Instructional Plan □ Learner Profiles □ Personalized Learning Plans □ Other:		
WHY: WHAT I HOPE TO LEARN AND/OR ACCOMPLISH	RESOURCES NEEDED	RESOURCES NEEDED

IMPLEMENT – 5 E MODEL

ENGAGE: (hook, rationale, anticipatory set)	EXPLORE: (build background knowledge)	EXPLAIN: (instructional components)
ELABORATE: (application of learning)	EVALUATE: (assessment of learning)	STUDENT REFLECTION: On learning & on learning process

REFLECT

LIKES / HIGHLIGHTS	CHALLENGES / THINGS TO CHANGE	WHAT WILL I USE AGAIN? NEXT STEPS?

WHAT I LEARNED / HOW I KNOW	
IMPACT ON TEACHER	IMPACT ON STUDENTS

NEXT STEPS FOR PLANNING IN THIS GOAL AREA

ACTION PLAN SAMPLE

GENIUS HOUR LAUNCH PLAN

ACTION PLAN

NAME: Dave N. **DATE:** 1-20-2015 **ROLE/ASSIGNMENT:** ELA Teacher

MY LEARNING GOALS

GOAL AREA		SPECIFIC STRATEGY OR PRACTICE
☐ Using Learner Data ☐ Personalized Learning Plans ☑ Student Driven Project Based Learning ☑ Flexible Spaces	☐ Blended Learning ☐ Flexible Instruction ☐ Other:	**Genius Hour** - Dedicated, and semistructured, time for student passion project and pursuits.

PLAN

WHAT AM I GOING TO DO?	WHEN AM I GOING TO DO IT?	WHERE AM I GOING TO DO IT? (COURSE, SECTION, CONTEXT)
☐ Instructional Plan ☐ Learner Profiles ☐ Personalized Learning Plans ☑ Other: Genius Hour Launch Event Plan. Also need to plan basic Genius Hour structures, timeframes, and the templates for students.	I would like to implement Genius Hour at the beginning and through-out 3rd quarter. The launch event would be on the first Friday in 3rd quarter.	With both of my English I classes.

WHY: WHAT I HOPE TO LEARN AND/OR ACCOMPLISH	RESOURCES NEEDED	RESOURCES NEEDED
I hope to enable higher levels of engagement and self-directed learning. I hope to facilitate my students' capacity to link learning outcomes from core content to their personal interests, passions and goals.	Models, videos to show kids the concept, documents & templates for student planning process, assessment/reflection strategies, scheduled time to use the school Maker Space.	How will I manage this effectively? If I don't have expertise in a student's project area, how can we find support for the student's work, learning and project?

IMPLEMENT – 5 E MODEL

ENGAGE: (hook, rationale, anticipatory set)	EXPLORE: (build background knowledge)	EXPLAIN: (instructional components)
Launch Event: with video segments of Genius Hour from another school and samples of the types of projects other kids have completed. Survey of students' interests, passions and wonders. Provide quick overview of Genius Hour plan / process.	**Rotational Model:** Stations include: 2 Stations with Genius Hour Artifacts from actual students from other schools (set the bar high) 1 Station with GH video & Discussion Prompt, 1 Station with a brain-storming process, 1 Station with the student Project Planning Templates / Proposal Process.	**Mini-Lesson:** How to use the planning templates and project proposal process. **Instructional critique:** Teacher share models of filled out planning forms. Students critique models to show elements of strength and weakness.

GENIUS HOUR LAUNCH PLAN

IMPLEMENT – 5 E MODEL

ELABORATE: (application of learning)	EVALUATE: (assessment of learning)	STUDENT REFLECTION: On learning & on learning process
Application Task: Students start planning process using the planning forms. Must pitch idea to teacher before beginning the project process.	**Exit Ticket:** Prompt - What does Genius Hour mean to me? What are my hopes and fears about Genius Hour? (Ongoing monitoring of progress with GH logs and assessment of integrated learning outcomes.)	**Exit Ticket:** Prompt –Think about the process of learning today - the launch event, the station rotation, the minilesson, the critique session and the use of the planning templates. What did you like? What would you change? Why?

REFLECT

LIKES / HIGHLIGHTS	CHALLENGES / THINGS TO CHANGE	WHAT WILL I USE AGAIN? NEXT STEPS?
I like the excitement this generated for students, everyone really got into it. I liked (and was surprised by) the variety of topics students expressed as areas of interest. Students were receptive to using the project planning templates.	**Challenge:** I noticed some offtopic discussions at the stations during the rotational model. **Change:** I may consider demonstrating a discussionbased station and ask students to come up with norms for that type of station based on what they see in the demo.	Launch events to generate engagement, excitement, curiosity, motivation and questions. Rotational model, but with greater priming and norms. Exit tickets gave great insight about what students learned, how they are feeling and how they learned.

WHAT I LEARNED / HOW I KNOW

IMPACT ON TEACHER	IMPACT ON STUDENTS
• I was concerned about students not being able to come up with their own project idea. I feel reassured based on my observations, that with a small amount of structure and guidance, that they can guide their own learning. • I realize that my role may need to shift *from* "instructor" *to* "mentor" and "facilitator." • I learned that my students have big hopes but they are also hesitant and reluctant in the face of an open ended challenge. • I learned from their exit tickets that I will need to encourage, coach, mentor and support their process over time.	• Based on their responses in class and on the feedback from their exit tickets…. • Students were initially reluctant, hesitant and unsure. They are used to being told what to do. So, this seemed intimidating at first. • In their exit tickets, there were some fears that eluded to being able to complete a project successfully. However, this was balanced with their hopes to do really cool things.

NEXT STEPS FOR PLANNING IN THIS GOAL AREA

- Plan instructional critique session to create norms for discussion-based stations.
- Conference with students as they develop their project plans. Model project "pitch" process.
- Broker peer and adult experts to support various student projects.

WORLD CAFE PROTOCOL

WORLD CAFE

In this protocol for discussion, each table is assigned a topic, with a discussion prompt. Participants select the table and topic of their choice and discuss the topic and prompt for 5-10 minutes. Participants switch tables 3-4 times, selecting their top topics. It can feel a bit like "musical chairs," but with enough rotations, one usually gets their top choices of topics by the end. At each table, using chart or butcher paper, groups attempt to create a visual representation of their discussion, with minimal usage of words. Groups review and build on previous discussion visuals and share their final one.

TABLE DISCUSSION PROMPTS

WHAT

What is this practice or strategy, exactly?

WHAT

In your preliminary research, did you unveil any misconceptions about this practice or strategy?

WHY

How could this practice increase student agency and/or provide positive benefits?

WHO

How might this practice or strategy impact teachers, students or others?

HOW

In what ways have you already used or experienced this practice or strategy?

HOW

In what ways could you envision using this practice or strategy?

NEXT STEPS

What lingering questions do you have about this practice/strategy?

NEXT STEPS

Will you continue to explore and pursue this practice or strategy? If so, how?

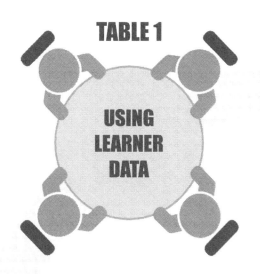

TABLE 1

USING LEARNER DATA

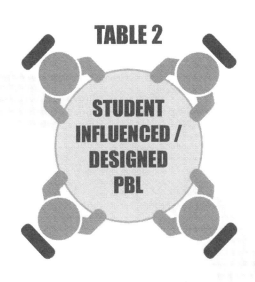

TABLE 2

STUDENT INFLUENCED / DESIGNED PBL

TABLE 3

PERSONALIZED LEARNING PLANS

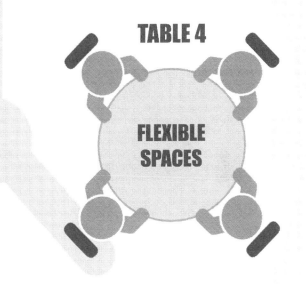

TABLE 4

FLEXIBLE SPACES

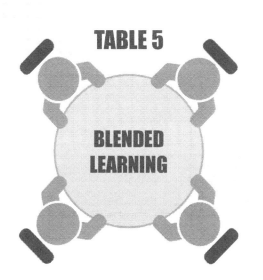

TABLE 5

BLENDED LEARNING

TABLE 6

FLEXIBLE INSTRUCTION

40457845R00030

Made in the USA
San Bernardino, CA
20 October 2016